Queries for Reflection

A **Study Guide Companion** to

Unlacing the Heart
Connecting With What Really Matters

Prepared by
Henry B. Freeman and **Colin Saxton**

Friends United Press

Friends United Press
101 Quaker Hill Drive
Richmond, IN 47374
friendspress@fum.org
shop.fum.org

ISBN 978-0-9962462-1-7

Jewish scholars call the books of Job, Proverbs, and Ecclesiastes, "Wisdom Literature," because they contain important reflections on the human condition and clarify how people ought to live in God's world.

Unlacing the Heart is wisdom literature.

—From the foreword, John Stewart, author/editor of *Bridges, Not Walls*

I experienced the joy
and privilege of being a
human chair with arms
to wrap around children
who did not have parents
to hold them.

—Henry B. Freeman

· Introduction ·

Unlacing the Heart is more than the title of a wonderful little book by Henry Freeman. May I suggest it is also a metaphor for something much deeper and an invitation to something much richer, at least for those of us who are willing?

Think for a moment about your own life. What would it mean to have your heart unlaced? What would widen and grow in you as it expanded? What shackles, barriers or protective shells would fall away as those ribbons round your heart were loosened? What do you imagine would be different in the way you related to others around you as your heart was increasingly set free?

For those of you reading *Unlacing the Heart* together and reflecting on these Queries as a group, how would "unlaced hearts" change the way you interact with one another? How would the content and character within a small fellowship be impacted over time if we could and would relate to one another in open-hearted ways?

The unlacing of our hearts is what happens when the barriers we have established around us begin to crumble, and we allow ourselves to authentically and vulnerably connect with another human being.

This unlacing occurs when the thick, callous hardness that has kept our hearts from being touched by another's suffering or pricked by another person's pain starts to soften as we share in their experience. And, of course, the unlacing of the heart most certainly occurs when we dare to feel and express that riskiest of all emotions—love. For while love leaves open the possibility our hearts may be broken or crushed, it is also the key to them swelling with life's deepest joy and highest good.

The unlacing of our hearts is what happens when the barriers we have established around us begin to crumble and we allow ourselves to authentically and vulnerably connect with another human being.

Within the stories from Henry Freeman's life comes an invitation to all of us to do more than be warmed by his experience of connecting with others. Even more, Henry is encouraging us to open our eyes and genuinely see the others we meet along our journey through life. These may be familiar faces—close friends, family members, and co-workers—people who we always notice but ones we may never have really known beyond a surface level. Further along the journey, we may also be blessed to encounter complete and unlikely strangers, just as Henry did through his life-changing encounter with Alfredo. Especially in the lives of the forgotten, the overlooked, and ignored, we may stumble across a person who heals something in us we did not even know was broken.

And maybe most hopefully, in our willingness to see others who are often unseen and move toward them with open-hearted grace and compassion, we will, in fact, come to meet Jesus himself. If my own experience is any indication, it is through encounters with the least of these that I find myself in the Presence of Christ and where my heart is increasingly set free.

This small pamphlet of Queries is an invitation from Henry and me to use *Unlacing the Heart* as an entry point into your own life stories. We have included queries that relate to the chapters from Henry's book and have added Bible passages, with an additional set of queries, to broaden the connections to the larger story of God's work throughout human history.

In some instances, the stories you uncover will be joyful and empowering. Other stories, grounded in personal tragedy and pain, may also emerge and prompt an inner journey into a place you would rather not go. In either case, we encourage you to interact with the stories and the queries in a way and a pace that seems right to you. In my own experience, there have been times when I have been most helped by wrestling deeply with a set of queries and pushing myself to share as honestly and vulnerably as I know how with others. At other times, however, it has been best to let the queries steep over time, waiting patiently and quietly for a deeper, more hidden work to happen before sharing my reflections and insight with others or not. Sometimes, a query evokes a response that is meant only for you.

Regardless of the stories uncovered, they are your stories and yours alone. They are part of your life journey as a person and one of your deepest points of connection to other people, the world, and to God. As you remember these stories and reflect on their meaning before God and others, may your heart be warmed, stretched, and even unlaced along the way.

Colin Saxton
General Secretary
Friends United Meeting

Alfredo

Photo by Henry B. Freeman

· Queries ·

Why Queries—and (for those of you who are not Quaker)
What Exactly is a Query?

In the summer of 2015, fourteen friends gathered in Brevard, North Carolina, to discuss a book suggested by one of the group's members. The book was *Unlacing the Heart*, and the person who recommended it is my sister, Kae Freeman Parker.

The fourteen friends (known affectionately as "Group") have a thirty year history of meeting one evening each week to discuss a book or topic of interest. Originally a Bible Study organized by a local Presbyterian Church, Group's membership evolved over the years to include people at various points on their faith journeys (ranging from active church members representing several denominations to people questioning and challenged on their spiritual pilgrimage). As might be expected for a gathering of people who have met together weekly for much of their adult lives, members of Group bring to the table a wide range of life experiences, including those of married and single people, parents and grandparents, teachers, social workers, caregivers, pastors, a retired theology professor, and a farmer.

When I learned from my sister that *Unlacing the Heart* was the topic for discussion, I was intrigued to hear about the lively conversation and depth of questions that surfaced during Group's introduction to the stories in my book. Of particular interest was how the stories shared by a Quaker of forty years standing resonated so deeply with people from a wide array of backgrounds, faith perspectives, and life experiences.

One day, as my sister shared with me the depth of discussion and the questions being addressed, I commented about the wonderful Queries lifted up by Group's members. What I soon learned was that the term "Query" has a rich history within my faith community dating back over three centuries.

The use of Queries is deeply embedded in the faith and practice of Quakers dating back over three centuries. Queries are rarely embraced as a form of spiritual practice outside the "small world" of the Religious Society of Friends (also known as Quakers).

Queries are rarely embraced as a form of spiritual practice outside the "small world" of the Religious Society of Friends (also known as Quakers). As members of Group struggled for a definition of "Query," I added to the confusion by finding that a term that is widely embraced by Friends is very difficult to define and explain to those from other faith traditions.

Realizing that these fourteen friends (none of whom are Quaker) and I may have uncovered a "gift to be shared" with those from other religious traditions, I called on Thomas Hamm, Earlham College's Quaker historian and archivist, and asked if he would help explain to non-Friends the rich history of Queries within our faith community and their role in the faith and practice of modern-day Friends.

The Use of Queries among Early Friends

The history of Queries and their function within the Religious Society of Friends can be traced back to the 1650s. At that time, Queries served two primary functions. Some Queries were specifically designed to gather and provide information about routine organizational matters—noting what ministers and elders had died during the past year; how many Meetings (Quaker terminology for a local congregation) had been established; and other statistical information about the state of what Friends at times refer to as "the Society". The second function of Queries gave Friends a way, as a religious body, to gauge how "Truth prospered" at the local Meeting level. In effect, the lifting up of a Query that addressed an issue of great importance and concern of Friends (such as adherence to "plainness of dress" or the avoidance of "worldly diversions," such as dancing and taverns) served as a way to "keep Friends in line" through the encouragement of righteous and "right-ordered" living.

Friends Understanding and Use of Queries Today

Unlike three centuries ago, Queries are rarely used by Friends in the twenty-first century to admonish bad behavior or try to convince another person of the rightness of one's own position or belief. Rather, a well-crafted and worded Query is intended to discern and deepen "my" or "our" understanding of a situation through inward reflection on one's beliefs, attitudes, and actions.

At first glance, the Queries presented in the following pages may appear to be little more than a series of short and straightforward questions. (Webster's dictionary, in fact, identifies a query as simply another term for "question" and the familiar question mark symbol itself is, at times, referred to as a query.)

Within the Quaker community, however, a Query has a much deeper spiritual purpose and function. Rather than simply a question designed to promote discussion or conversation, the "lifting up" or "raising" of a Query by or among Friends is a practice whose purpose is to encourage a deep level of "inward reflection" that may (or may not) be verbally shared with others. Indeed, the freedom to "share" or "not share" one's thoughts and feelings in response to a Query is critical, since the very purpose of a Query is to promote self-reflection and discernment rather than discussion or agreement within a group.

The reason agreement with or affirmation by others is not the objective of a Query is very simple. A Query does not illicit or draw forth from an individual a "right" or "wrong" answer. The "truth" to be found in a person's response to a Query is what the person receives through his or her reflection on the Query's meaning as it relates to their personal life and relationship with God.

Another characteristic of a Query as understood by Friends is that its focus is not as much on a "fact" as it is on the experience of the person who is embracing and exploring the Query. For this reason, the Queries presented in the following pages will not (if carefully read) lead to a discussion of "Henry Freeman's experience in El Salvador" or "a homeless man named Alfredo" but rather how the stories shared in *Unlacing the Heart* resonate with deeply powerful stories found and experienced in the heart of the reader.

Henry Freeman
Author, *Unlacing the Heart*

Every time I held Mimi, a five-year old who sought comfort each day in my overgrown North American lap, my doubts and fears began to slide away.

—Henry B. Freeman

• Introduction to Unlacing the Heart •

Chapter Summary

Henry Freeman's life was transformed by three distinctly different friends: a well-known theologian and author; a mentor as comfortable with a bag lady who lived on the streets as he was with a wealthy Yale student with the world at his fingertips; and a homeless man named Alfredo who asked nothing more than that Henry sit down beside him and be his friend.

Selected Quotes

"The marvelous thing about learning from a story is that a story never ends, so our learning from it need not end either."—Parker J. Palmer

"One of the most visible hats I wear is that of a fundraising consultant. As is true of most professions, a rather generic title like 'fundraiser' tells you very little about whom I am and what I actually do."

Scripture Reading

Luke 4:14-30, Jesus rejected at Nazareth

Jesus' message and ministry often met resistance from others who were tempted to limit him to their perception of his upbringing and qualifications or their expectations around who and what a Messiah should be.

- In what ways have I felt limited in my service for God?

"'Truly I tell you,' he continued, 'no prophet is accepted in his hometown.'"

It took great courage for Jesus to re-script other people's image of him as only "Joseph's son."

- When have I experienced others, or myself, doing something similarly courageous? How did this make me feel?

Reflection

With news of his public ministry beginning to spread across the countryside, Jesus comes home to the family, friends, and familiar surroundings of Galilee. Standing in the synagogue to speak, he utters powerful and prophetic words and a message unexpected, especially by those who have known him as "Joseph's son."

Queries

Our stories

- How have I experienced "my story" living on in the life of another person?
- How has someone else's story "lived on" within me?

Our role in life: The "hat" each of us wears

- How does the "hat" I wear reflect who I am as a person?
- In what ways does the hat I wear shape how others view and relate to me?

Notes

What heart-centered stories, lessons, and memories are unlaced as I reflect on these Queries and my personal life journey?

_____

_____

_____

_____

_____

_____

_____

_____

_____

_____

_____

_____

_____

_____

_____

_____

_____

_____

_____

_____

_____

_____

_____

_____

_____

_____

_____

_____

_____

· Chapter 1 ·
The Journey to El Salvador

Chapter Summary

When full of self-doubt and a level of fear that had taken him to a very dangerous place psychologically, emotionally, and physically, Henry found comfort and compassion in a community of children who asked nothing more of him than that he be authentically present with them and be part of their lives.

Selected Quotes

"In El Salvador I experienced the joy and privilege of being a human chair with arms to wrap around children who did not have parents to hold them . . . I learned some of my most important lessons from children whose whispers and giggles woke me up each morning."

". . . a new way of viewing the world began to unfold within me and become an increasingly powerful presence in my life."

"One gift of childhood is the ability to call other people away from their fears and self-doubts."

Scripture Reading

Luke 18:15-17, Little children and Jesus

People were also bringing babies to Jesus for him to place his hands on them. When the disciples saw this, they rebuked them. But Jesus called the children to him and said, "Let the little children come to me, and do not hinder them, for the kingdom of God belongs to such as these."

Reflection

Unlike his first followers, Jesus embraced and welcomed the children right into the center of religious activities and social occasions. Holding them up as an example for others, Jesus suggests it may be the youngest among us who are most eager and able to receive the Kingdom of God.

Queries

A new way of viewing the world

- What one experience in my life most radically altered or shaped my view of the world?

- How has that experience shaped how I relate to other people?

Pushing away fear

- Where do I turn to find comfort and compassion during the times I am experiencing fear, loneliness, and despair?

- How do fear and hate find their way into my life?

- Who are the people that are fearful of me? Why might they fear me?

Lessons to be learned from children

- What lessons about life have I, as an adult, learned from children?

- How have these lessons impacted how I live my life as an adult?

Little children and Jesus

- What childlike qualities allow us to see and experience the Kingdom of God most deeply?

- What in life erodes or hinders my ability to think and act in childlike ways before God?

Notes

What heart-centered stories, lessons, and memories are unlaced as I reflect on these Queries and my personal life journey?

_____

_____

_____

_____

_____

_____

_____

_____

_____

_____

_____

_____

_____

_____

· Chapter 2 ·
Confessions of Good Deeds

Chapter Summary

Sister Margaret had a gift for seeing what Quakers refer to as "that of God in every person," including a young soldier others believed she had every reason to fear and hate.

Selected Quotes

"There is only one way out of fear and that is love."—William Sloane Coffin

"Very simply put, if the soldiers were invisible to you perhaps in some magical way you would be invisible to them."—Henry Freeman

"I have never intentionally hurt anyone."—young soldier

Scripture Reading

Luke 7:36-50, Jesus anointed by a sinful woman

Reflection

A nice religious gathering is unexpectedly interrupted by an unwelcome intruder, at least from the perspective of the Pharisee. Jesus the Rabbi sees a woman in need of love and forgiveness. As Christ welcomes her in that moment, the woman responds by lavishing love upon him and finds the freedom to act as one who is acceptable to God.

"Then Jesus said to her, 'Your sins are forgiven.' The other guests began to say among themselves, 'Who is this who even forgives sins?' Jesus said to the woman, 'Your faith has saved you; go in peace.'"

Queries

Confessions of good deeds—or sins

- Where in my life do I find the opportunity to hear confessions of good deeds?

- Who is a "Sister Margaret" in my life? What lessons have I learned from that person?

Invisibility

- We have all had the experience of being invisible to another person. What did I learn from that experience of "invisibility?"

Jesus anointed by a sinful woman

- Jesus consistently sees and moves toward people whom others overlook, ignore, or turn their backs on. Who are the people who are invisible to me?

- What do I need from God to have grace-healed eyes that will allow me to see as Christ sees others?

- When have I experienced being unconditionally welcomed by Christ, especially when I have felt or been told I am unacceptable?

- What keeps me from expressing my love for Christ as freely as the woman in the story?

Notes

What heart-centered stories, lessons, and memories are unlaced as I reflect on these Queries and my personal life journey?

_____

_____

_____

_____

_____

_____

_____

_____

_____

_____

_____

_____

_____

_____

_____

_____

_____

_____

_____

_____

_____

_____

_____

_____

_____

_____

_____

· Chapter 3 ·
A Mother and Child by the Side of the Road

Chapter Summary

In a short five-minute ride down a mountainside in El Salvador, Henry had the privilege of sharing a special moment—one parent with another.

Selected Quotes

"Like dangling pieces of rope, the child's arms and legs swayed in rhythm to each of the woman's small, cautious steps."

". . . for most of us, happiness sits on the other side of our walls waiting patiently for us to open our doors to the joy and pain of the world around us."

Scripture Reading

Romans 12:9-18, Love

Reflection

After spending the first eleven chapters focused on theology in the book of *Romans*, the writer Paul gets very practical and offers ordinary advice for living an extraordinary life before God, in harmony with Christian brothers and sisters and for the sake of a hurting world. At the heart of this practical advice is the call to rejoice in hope—to find and choose joy—even in the midst of hardship and pain.

"If it is possible, as far as it depends on you, live at peace with everyone."

Queries

Finding joy and meaning in one's life

- How is it possible to find authentic happiness and joy when sharing in another person's pain and suffering?

- What must be present for me to live what I consider to be a "meaningful life?"

Parenthood

- The child-parent relationship is something that all human beings experience in life—some of those experiences are nurturing and affirming, and others can be very negative. In what ways do I bring my experience of childhood "with me" in my relationship with others?

Love

- What are the sources of joy in my life? How can I best share this joy with others?

- What do I, or can I, do to keep hope alive—especially when I see (or experience) so much pain and suffering?

Notes

What heart-centered stories, lessons, and memories are unlaced as I reflect on these Queries and my personal life journey?

· **Chapter 4** ·
Seeing Relationships Through a Different Lens

Chapter Summary

Building relationship is often described as being at the heart of what we do regardless of our profession or primary role in life—whether we are a fundraiser, caregiver, insurance salesman, teacher, or pastor. But what is the true nature of our relationship with most of the people we meet? Is what we define as a relationship with another person often simply filling our head with facts and information about that person and who we want them to "be," or what we want them to "do for us?"

Selected Quotes

"Perhaps how we view others determines how they view us."

"The sad truth is that many people in my profession (and, most likely, yours) never move beyond the facts they have gathered in how they see the people with whom they believe they have a meaningful relationship."

Scripture Reading

Philippians 3:3-11, No confidence in the flesh

Reflection

As a servant-leader in the church, the Apostle Paul had a long list of credentials that he could brandish to exert his influence, push an agenda, or shape discussion. Those around him knew his background, training, and

"But whatever were gains to me I now consider loss for the sake of Christ. What is more, I consider everything a loss because of the surpassing worth of knowing Christ Jesus my Lord, for whose sake I have lost all things."

experience. As he labored for them and among them, however, did they also know the deepest longing of his heart and his true motivation?

Queries

Knowing another person

- What are the barriers to really "knowing" another person and having another person really know me?

- If I could "wave a magic wand," how would I change the level and quality of my relationships with some of the people I know a lot "about," but do not really "know?"

- Virtually all human beings have some relationships in which they don't feel "safe" to share who they are at a deep level. With such a person, how can I build a relationship that is open and honest at a level that is respectful and appropriate?

No confidence in the flesh

- What are the obvious things people know about me?

- What are the most important matters of the heart that I wish others truly knew?

- If I could exchange all of my past achievements and accomplishments for one future hope to be realized in my life, what would it be?

Notes

What heart-centered stories, lessons, and memories are unlaced as I reflect on these Queries and my personal life journey?

· **Chapter 5** ·
Steak and Asparagus with Margaret

Chapter Summary

Wearing his hat as a fundraiser, Henry entered Margaret's life as a professional person who viewed their time together as one more item he needed to check off on a very important and hectic schedule. He left his evening with Margaret as a person whose life was transformed by an invitation to join her in a sacred space, where all she asked was for his presence at a very vulnerable time in her life.

Selected Quotes

"My goal was simply to 'keep in touch' in a way that might open the door for a future conversation about her estate plans."

"Henry, now be honest with me. Do you like fresh asparagus?"

"Thank you, God, for having Henry here so I have someone to talk to."

"I learned this morning that I am dying of cancer . . . And now, Henry, what is it that you want to talk about."

Scripture Reading

Mark 10:46-52, Blind Bartemaus receives his sight

"'What do you want me to do for you?' Jesus asked him. The blind man said, 'Rabbi, I want to see.' 'Go,' said Jesus, 'your faith has healed you.' Immediately he received his sight and followed Jesus along the road."

Reflection

As Jesus journeys from Jericho to Jerusalem, a large and noisy crowd presses in around him from all sides. Even as he prepares to face into his most intense season of ministry, Jesus still hears the solitary voice of a blind man calling out for mercy. Though others try to silence and conceal him, Jesus calls the man forward and asks, "What do you want me to do for you?"

Queries

Our busy lives and agendas

- How has my "professional hat" or role in life gotten in the way of my being the person I want and desire to be in my relationship with another person?

- What can I do to give me the strength and sensitivity to enter the life of another person as a guest, rather than as a person driven by an agenda and the hectic life I so often lead?

Vulnerability

- When have I had the experience of someone being thankful to God for my presence at a vulnerable time in their life?

- What invitations into another person's vulnerable space have I missed or not heard?

- We have all been wounded in some way by invitations we extended that were not heard or were turned away. What did these experiences teach me about myself and others?

- When has simply "being present" been the only gift I was able to offer another person? Was the gift of my presence "enough?"

Blind Bartemaus receives his sight

- In what ways and at what times have I experienced Christ coming near to me?

- If Jesus were to appear to me now and ask me, "what do you want me to do for you," what would I say?

- What can I learn from Jesus' example in this story?

Notes

What heart-centered stories, lessons, and memories are unlaced as I reflect on these Queries and my personal life journey?

_____

_____

_____

_____

_____

_____

_____

_____

_____

_____

_____

_____

_____

· Chapter 6 ·
Alfredo, My Friend and Teacher

Chapter Summary

To the world, Alfredo was a man with little value: a beggar with nothing he could possibly offer to the world. Alfredo was, however, a person who offered far more to Henry than was apparent to those who saw him each day with his hand held out on a street corner in El Salvador. He was a man who invited Henry into his life, asking nothing more than the opportunity to sit side by side as friends.

Selected Quotes

"Our friendship was based on nothing more than Alfredo's single question and the simple act of sitting together with an arm wrapped around each other's shoulder."

"How are you, my brother? I am well, and you?"

"The most important gift you can give me is to see me as a human being who, like you, has a story to share but few people who will listen."—Alfredo

"Love the Lord your God with all your heart and with all your soul and with all your strength and with all your mind and, love your neighbor as yourself."

Scripture Reading

Luke 10:25-37, The Parable of the Good Samaritan

Reflection

When an expert in the Law tries to give Jesus a religious test over how it is we inherit eternal life, Christ turns the question back on him. "What does the book say?" Jesus asks. The Law expert responds rightly that we are to "Love God and love our neighbor," with all sincerity and passion. And then, in an opening that moves a familiar teaching to a deeper and more transforming place, Jesus tells an unexpected story about who really is our neighbor.

Queries

Friendship

- Who is an "Alfredo" in my life—a person who asks nothing more than that I be truly and authentically present as their friend?

- At what point have I encountered a total stranger and seen or felt the presence of God in their life and in the relationship we entered together?

- When have I been the lonely and vulnerable person through whom someone experienced God's presence in their life?

The Parable of the Good Samaritan

- When has someone treated me as their "neighbor?"

- In light of Jesus' parable, who is my neighbor?

- How might Jesus tell this story in our time?

Notes

What heart-centered stories, lessons, and memories are unlaced as I reflect on these Queries and my personal life journey?

_____

_____

_____

_____

_____

_____

_____

_____

_____

_____

_____

_____

_____

_____

_____

_____

_____

_____

_____

_____

_____

_____

_____

_____

_____

_____

_____

_____

_____

· **Chapter 7** ·
A Space to be Vulnerable: A Gift from Henri Nouwen

Chapter Summary

In Professor Nouwen's class, Henry was asked a very simple question: What does it mean to "be present" with another person?

In that moment, he was invited into the life of a man whose own woundedness and vulnerability allowed him to speak to the hearts of hundreds of thousands of people around the world through his books and his writing. To Henry, however, it was a deeply personal invitation to find and explore within himself a "safe place" where wounds can be healed and lives are transformed.

Selected Quotes

"A space to be vulnerable is not a gift we can learn or acquire with our head. It is a gift that only exists when shared heart-to-heart with another."

"A space to be vulnerable is where at various points on my life journey I return and, metaphorically speaking, sit in Henri Nouwen's class again and experience the same vulnerability and acceptance I found that day . . . A space I returned to twenty years later and found the strength to tell Earlham's president I was leaving to live in the laundry of an orphanage in El Salvador. Something college vice-presidents just don't do . . ."

Scripture Reading

Luke 24:13-35, On the road to Emmaus

"They asked each other, 'Were not our hearts burning within us while he talked with us on the road and opened the Scriptures to us?'"

Reflection

Downcast at the news of Jesus' death, two disciples wander toward Emmaus when the Messiah joins them along the way. Inexplicably, they do not recognize him in their midst, even as they describe him and his message in vivid detail. Over the course of their conversation, however, Jesus creates a space where these two open up about their broken hearts and dashed dreams. They even dare to share a bit of news—Jesus' tomb was empty, and he may be alive. Over dinner and brief bible study, their eyes opened to his presence; their hearts were kindled with hope; and their lives were turned completely around.

Queries

A space to be vulnerable

- When in my life have I been invited into a safe space for vulnerability?

- What was the impact of that experience on my life?

- Human beings yearn for "safe spaces" in their relationships with others. All of us, however, have at one time or another, found that what we thought was a safe space for vulnerability was not. How has such an experience impacted my ability—or desire—to come out from behind my walls and be vulnerable again?

- When have I been empowered to break out of my expected role and do something that could easily be misunderstood—or viewed as silly or stupid—by those around me?

On the road to Emmaus

- When have I experienced God turning my life in a completely new direction?

- How did God get me ready for this?

- Something about Jesus caused the disciples' hearts to be kindled with passion, joy, and love. When have I experienced something like this? What inspired those feelings?

- Jesus joined these two dejected people on a journey toward hope. How might I do something similar for people in my life?

Notes

What heart-centered stories, lessons, and memories are unlaced as I reflect on these Queries and my personal life journey?

_____

_____

_____

_____

_____

_____

_____

_____

_____

_____

_____

_____

_____

_____

_____

_____

_____

_____

_____

_____

_____

_____

_____

_____

_____

· Chapter 8 ·
Herbert A. Cahoon and Mary

Chapter Summary

Herb Cahoon was a person very comfortable in his own skin: a person whose goal in life was to uncover the dreams to be found in the rest of us. He was also a person who was as comfortable entering the life of a homeless woman named Mary as he was listening to the life story of a Yale student born into a wealthy family with the world at his fingertips.

Selected Quotes

"As my toddler-aged twins soon learned, Herb was a 'funny old man' who would show up at a child's birthday party at the invitation of a two-year old."

"One of Herb's greatest gifts was the ability to see in people a dream that could change the world. It didn't matter how idealistic the dream, Herb would make it appear to be rationale and doable."

"When Mary walked out of Dwight Hall that day, she was still a bag lady whose day-to-day life would never change . . . Mary did, however, have in Herb Cahoon someone who was willing and able to be present with her for that hour of her life . . . As far as I know, Herb was never too busy to see Mary—a person who sheltered a special place in her life that only he was allowed to enter."

Scripture Reading

John 4:7-26 and *4:39-42*, Jesus talks with a Samaritan woman

"Yet a time is coming and has now come when the true worshipers will worship the Father in the Spirit and in truth, for they are the kind of worshipers the Father seeks. God is spirit, and his worshipers must worship in the Spirit and in truth."

Reflection

In an utterly surprising encounter, Rabbi Jesus enters into a deep conversation with a Samaritan woman who is drawing water from a well. The Samaritans generally despised by Jews, and this particular Samaritan was probably also were ostracized by her own people, due to her life choices. Even so, Jesus engages her, takes her questions and concerns seriously, and sees something of value in her—when no one else, including herself, probably did. Inspired by his message and acceptance, she becomes a channel for grace and faith for others.

Queries

Transformational people in our lives

- Who is a Herb Cahoon in my life—a person gifted at finding what is good in me and other people? A person who joyfully responds to the birthday party invitation of a two-year old or finds time for the "Marys" of our world?

- How has a Herb Cahoon in my life influenced the person I am today, and shaped my view of the world and other people?

- When have I been invited into the life of a person like Mary? What kept me from accepting such an invitation—or enabled me to do so?

- How has God's, or another person's, acceptance of me freed me to be of help to others?

- Is there someone in my life to whom I could extend this kind of grace?

- How might I go about sharing grace with others in a way that is safe for them?

Notes

What heart-centered stories, lessons, and memories are unlaced as I reflect on these Queries and my personal life journey?

_____

_____

_____

_____

_____

_____

_____

_____

_____

_____

_____

_____

_____

· Chapter 9 ·
Learning to Fail:
Serving Soup and Building Dreams

Chapter Summary

Henri Nouwen and Herb Cahoon believed in Henry, not because of any future success they envisioned, but because each of them wanted to be supportive of Henry's life journey. Their "true gift" was their authentic "presence" at an important yet vulnerable point in his life. The same was true for another Henry's gift to Jane, when he invited her to the Community Soup Kitchen: a place where she would "not be lonely anymore."

Selected Quotes

"While in my eyes I saw failure, Herb—in his own magical way—saw success!. . . Totally ignoring my original goal, Herb began spreading the word that Henry Freeman knows how to raise money!"

"In that small magical moment, Jane and her friends learned what it meant to be welcomed into a community . . . They also experienced what it means to be welcomed unconditionally into another person's life."

Scripture Reading

Hebrews 11:1-2; 8-16; 39-40, By faith

"Now faith is confidence in what we hope for and assurance about what we do not see. This is what the ancients were commended for."

Reflection

Through absolute trust in a God he could not see, Abraham set out on a journey toward a home he had never visited. Over the entire course of his life, Abraham continued to act in hope as he and others pressed on toward a God-inspired vision of a new and better world. Though his faith was never fully realized in his life, it continues to find expression and completion in all who share the same radical trust in God.

Queries

The gifts we receive—and give

- What is the most precious and important gift I have received from another person?

- What has been the impact of that gift on my life and the lives of others?

- Henry's invitation to Jane to be his guest at the Community Soup Kitchen was a simple yet profoundly meaningful gesture. If I were invited by Henry, what impact could this invitation have on my life?

- What vision has God called me to pursue with relentless faithfulness?

- How am I seeing it come to pass—at least in part?

- Unlike Abraham, many people see their faith and hope crushed. Who around me would benefit from my encouragement and support for their faithful pursuit of God?

Notes

What heart-centered stories, lessons, and memories are unlaced as I reflect on these Queries and my personal life journey?

_____

_____

_____

_____

_____

_____

_____

_____

_____

_____

_____

_____

_____

_____

_____

_____

_____

_____

_____

_____

_____

_____

_____

_____

_____

_____

_____

_____

_____

· Chapter 10 ·
Henri and Herb:
A Study in Contradictions

Chapter Summary

Herb and Henri were two very different people who shared the same gift for "being present" in the lives of others. One was a Catholic priest deeply committed to following Jesus. The other was an agnostic, who viewed the world through a very practical and secular lens, where what a person believed was of little value and how a person lived was what really mattered.

Selected Quotes

"Often our life journey weaves together individuals who are a study in contradictions . . . people whose lives bring to the table very similar gifts, yet do so from completely different places of strength."

"In spite of his success and fame, Henri Nouwen was a man who spent his life searching for community but often tried to find it in the wrong places."

Scripture Reading

Acts 9: 1-31, Saul's conversion

Reflection

On the road to Damascus, Saul of Tarsus has a life-changing encounter with the resurrected Christ. In the process of having his whole life re-oriented and redirected by the Holy Spirit, a couple of instrumental friends come alongside him to encourage, counsel, and stand with this former adversary of

"At once he began to preach in the synagogues that Jesus is the Son of God. All those who heard him were astonished and asked, 'Isn't he the man who raised havoc in Jerusalem among those who call on this name?'"

the church. Through their willingness to listen to God and willingness to trust Saul's sincerity, Ananias and Barnabas make a courageous and transformative investment in one of the key future leaders of the church—at a time when others would not.

Queries

- Along my life journey, where have I found sustenance and support through my relationship with a person (perhaps a person like Herb or Henri) whose beliefs and views of God are very different from my own?

- When in my life have I searched in the wrong places for a place to call "home?" What within me led me on such a journey?

- Where now, at this point in my life, do I find community and people with whom I can take down my walls and truly and authentically welcome others?

- All of us have relationships and "spaces" in our lives where, to varying degrees, we "pretend" to experience community. How does this experience of "pretending"—so common in today's world—shape my understanding of the following words by Henri Nouwen:

   > "The roots of loneliness are very deep and cannot be touched by optimistic advertisements, substitute love images, or social togetherness. They find their food in the suspicion that there is no one who cares and offers love without conditions, and no place where we can be vulnerable without being used."—Henri Nouwen, *Reaching Out*

- Who are the saints who have made a sacrificial investment in my life?

- Has there been a time when I have felt called to stand-up for (or stand alongside) someone, when others would not?

- What was that experience like?

Notes

What heart-centered stories, lessons, and memories are unlaced as I reflect on these Queries and my personal life journey?

_____

_____

_____

_____

_____

_____

_____

_____

_____

_____

_____

_____

_____

· **Chapter 11** ·
Lorenzo

Chapter Summary

Suddenly, Henry found himself in a very different world. A place where he was scared, felt helpless, and very much alone. Then, in the dim light of a candle, a friend joined him. A friend named Henri, who, like another Henry twenty years earlier on a very different journey with a young woman named Jane, welcomed the author into a place where he was no longer alone.

Selected Quotes

"Within moments my lighted candle discovered a photograph of hands held together ready to embrace a drink of water or a crumb of bread. It was a simple yet powerful image I had seen twenty years earlier at Yale during a time in my life far removed from the little room I now shared with my unknown roommate."

"While I no longer remember all the details of the letter I do remember my opening words, 'Thank you, Henri, for being here,' . . . With regret, I never sent Henri the letter I wrote on that lonely night in El Salvador."

"[At Daybreak among Henri's friends] there was lots of laughter and joyful conversation about a man fondly remembered for the love in his heart. A man who made the decision to leave the scholarly life of Yale and Harvard to spend the last years of his life living with people who could not read his books and couldn't care less about his fame."

Scripture Reading

Psalm 63:1-8, Psalm of David

"Because your love is better than life,
my lips will glorify you.
I will praise you as long as I live, and in your name I will lift up my hands."

Reflection

In Hebrew, the act of remembering means "to make present." As David remembers God, in the depth of his despair, the very presence of God brings comfort, courage, and peace. Like a long cool drink of water, God satisfies David's thirst for company and strength by reminding him of past provision and current help in a time of need.

Queries

The gift of being present

- At what point have I experienced the "presence" of another person—through a book, a memory, a gift, or shared object—that provided me with great comfort at a fearful time in my life?

- To whom do I turn when I need the presence of a person who—as Henri Nouwen found when living in a community of people who "could not read his books"—sees the "me" that lives behind my walls—the person who is easily identified by a label, title, or line on a job resume?

- To whom do I turn when overwhelmed by fear?

- Is the comfort I experience grounded in something that person "does for me," or more from the authentic "presence" that person shares with me at a fearful time in my life?

- How do I actively remember God's provision in my life and earnestly seek God's presence now?

- What are the sources of loneliness and fear in my life?

- How is God enabling me to overcome these?

Notes

What heart-centered stories, lessons, and memories are unlaced as I reflect on these Queries and my personal life journey?

_____

_____

_____

_____

_____

_____

_____

_____

_____

_____

_____

_____

_____

_____

_____

· **Chapter 12** ·
A Final Kiss on an Old Man's Head

Chapter Summary

At the end of an evening of good conversation and shared memories, Henry told his mentor what an impact he had had on his life. He then kissed Herb on top of his head and said, for the first time, "I love you." The next morning, Herb died. He was 91 years old.

Selected Quotes

"Then, on David and Sara's thirtieth birthday, the phone was silent. 'Old Man Cahoon' forgot to call."

"He had lived a good life."

". . . I began to realize that what I have to share . . . is not what we learn with our heads but a gift we receive with our hearts. It is the gift of being invited into another person's life, an invitation to be 'present' in a vulnerable space where our walls come down and our masks are taken off."

Scripture Reading

Acts 20:17-38, Paul's farewell to Ephesian elders

Reflection

After devoting so much time and energy to building up the church in Ephesus, the Apostle Paul realizes he must now turn his attention toward Jerusalem. His days serving them are finished and he will not be returning to

"In everything I did, I showed you that by this kind of hard work we must help the weak, remembering the words the Lord Jesus himself said: 'It is more blessed to give than to receive.' " When Paul had finished speaking, he knelt down with all of them and prayed. They all wept as they embraced him and kissed him."

be among them again. Calling the leaders of the church together, Paul reminds them of all he had taught them, commits the fellowship to the faithful care of God and tenderly blesses them in prayer. Before departing, Paul and his friends grieve together over the shared loss they were facing.

Queries

Saying Goodbye

- What memories do I have of saying goodbye to someone who had a transformational impact on my life?

- What was the impact of that person on my life?

- When have I experienced the end of an important and life-giving relationship because God has called one of us to move on?

- How did I grieve this loss?

- Are there people in my life I would want to thank, in person, for their impact on my life, if I knew I would not see them again?

- What is stopping me from doing it now?

Notes

What heart-centered stories, lessons, and memories are unlaced as I reflect on these Queries and my personal life journey?

_____

_____

_____

_____

_____

_____

_____

_____

_____

_____

_____

_____

_____

· Chapter 13 ·
Connecting with What Really Matters
in Our Lives and Careers

Chapter Summary

Few of us can toss aside the things that weigh heavily on our daily lives—the paperwork, financial realities, and other persons' expectations. What we can control is our willingness and desire to genuinely and authentically be present with another person, for whatever time and in whatever space we occupy with them.

Selected Quotes

"It was through their stories that there emerged a deep and heartfelt connection to me and my journey as a person. It was in this safe place that they found in me a person who genuinely and authentically cared about them, as people who—like Alfredo—had stories to share but few people who would take the time to listen."

"What is most troubling is that what draws many of us to these professions (clergy, teachers, social workers, etc.)—the belief that we will connect with other people at a deeply meaningful level—is often not what we find and experience."

"The problem for most of us is that, too often, we enter the lives of another person with an agenda that narrowly defines the relationship around what we want to talk about rather than what is in the heart of the person we are meeting with. As a result, we have nice and cordial meetings that rarely get to the heart of a person's deepest feelings and passions."

"When all the people saw him walking and praising God, they recognized him as the same man who used to sit begging at the temple gate called Beautiful, and they were filled with wonder and amazement at what had happened to him."

Scripture Reading

Acts 3:1-10, Peter heals the crippled beggar

Reflection

At times, the "professional hat" we wear may impact what we want to receive out of a relationship we establish. On the other hand, that same "hat" can foster false hopes or unrealistic expectations by others, as they seek something from us in the relationship. Peter and John experienced this reality when a lame man saw them coming to minister in Jerusalem. Hoping for cash, the man is caught off guard when Peter and John look intently into his face. They see him—and instead of offering a few dollars that would make no lasting difference, they give him a gift of true healing, profound joy, and a new life.

Queries

When we are welcomed into another person's life

- What are the barriers I face and feel that make me hesitant to share what Henry calls "that sacred space" with another person, when they open the door to their life and invite me in?

- What one step can I take that empowers me to "leave my agenda at the door" and be more fully present in the time and space I share with another person?

- Who in my life is, or has been, my "best teacher" when it comes to being "fully present" in my relationship with other people?

- In the work of service or ministry, have I ever felt like someone was trying to use me? How did that make me feel?

- When someone tries to put their unreasonable hopes or expectations on me, how can I respond in a graceful and redemptive way?

- If someone is beginning to relate to me in a superficial way, is there something I can do that might direct us both to a deeper conversation and encounter?

Notes

What heart-centered stories, lessons, and memories are unlaced as I reflect on these Queries and my personal life journey?

· Epilogue ·
Finding Our Way to What Matters in Life

Chapter Summary

As Henry put words to paper for his book, he often drifted back into childhood memories and experiences from growing up in the rural south more than a half century earlier. Some of those memories were joyful and others very painful. All, however, served as the foundation for the stories he shares, his view of the world, and his journey as a Quaker and person of faith.

Selected Quotes

"In the safety of our home, my father asked the all-important question, 'Who is our neighbor, and what does it mean to love and respect that person?'"

"I never told my father—or anyone else—what happened that day, or how I felt when a stranger laughed at me for doing what I believed was right."

"It was in our childhood—both for good and for bad—that the seeds were planted for who my brother and I are today. Seeds grounded in a tension between the faith we gleaned from my father—a faith grounded in asking the hard questions—and the religious beliefs and attitudes that held sway in the world just beyond our front door."

Scripture Reading

Colossians 3:8-17, Rules for holy living

"Therefore, as God's chosen people, holy and dearly loved, clothe yourselves with compassion, kindness, humility, gentleness and patience. Bear with each other and forgive one another if any of you has a grievance against someone. Forgive as the Lord forgave you."

Reflection

Among those whose lives have been united with the Living Christ, a new fellowship is being created. It is an alternative community, bound together in a strong bond of peace, animated and united by the Holy Spirit in ways that transcend all of the human barriers we tend to erect between ourselves. Because Christ is all—and is in all—cultural, racial, social, economic, and gender distinctions do not alienate; rather, they simply add to the beauty of God's work among us. Through the powerful grace of God at work within us, and the disciplined practice of love, forgiveness and humility, the church is called to reflect the glory of God in all it does and says.

Queries

Neighbors in a complex and changing world

- Who in today's world is my neighbor, and what does it mean to love and respect that person?

- At what point in my life have I been laughed at for doing what I believed was right? What has been the impact on my life of that experience?

The role of faith in my life

- How does my faith—or lack of faith—lead me to address the hard questions in life?

- Which do I find to be the more powerful force in my journey as a person of faith: the questions (or Queries) my faith leads me to address; or the answers I have found within the faith community of which I am a member?

Rules for holy living

- What can I do to actively seek the unity of the church in my local fellowship?

- What would it look like if I and a few of my friends made "clothing ourselves with compassion, kindness, humility, gentleness and patience" a priority for our lives?

- How has God forgiven me?
- What, then, does it mean to "forgive others as God has forgiven me?"

Notes

What heart-centered stories, lessons, and memories are unlaced as I reflect on these Queries and my personal life journey?

_____

_____

_____

_____

_____

_____

_____

_____

_____

_____

_____

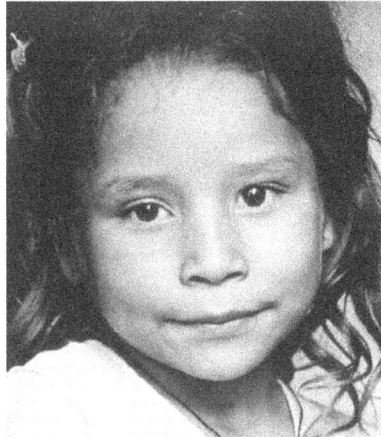

I was captivated by the eyes of a small girl.

—Henry B. Freeman

www.ingramcontent.com/pod-product-compliance
Lightning Source LLC
Chambersburg PA
CBHW081221020426
42331CB00012B/3067